The Spirituality Vol 1

The Spirituality Vol 1

The Natural Phenomenon That Is Spiritual Sight

JOSEPH GARCIA

Library of Congress Control Number: 2024914500

ISBN: 979-8-89228-188-1   (Paperback)
ISBN: 979-8-89228-187-4   (eBook)

Book Ordering Information:
Atticus Publishing
548 Market St PMB 70756
San Francisco, CA 94104
(888) 208-9296
info@atticuspublishing.com
www.atticuspublishing.com

Printed in the United States of America

Table of Contents

Caution: this book may open your spiritual sight

Preface

In the vast knowledge of human existence, a profound and timeless journey awaits us all—the quest for spiritual sight. It's a voyage into the depths of our consciousness, a path that reveals hidden layers of reality, and an exploration of our divine connection.

This book extends an invitation to embark on this sacred journey that transcends the boundaries of science and spirituality, space and time. It will guide you beyond your physical senses into the realm of the unseen, where the heart's wisdom takes center stage.

Within these pages, you'll uncover the mysteries of spiritual sight, blending ancient wisdom with modern science. You'll find practices and insights that can awaken your inner vision, allowing you to perceive the world with a fresh, profound perspective. You'll discover the keys to unlock your third eye through these words—an entrance to heightened awareness, expanded consciousness, and a deeper bond with the universe.

However, remember that this book is more than a mere guide. It's a mirror reflecting your immense potential. You are more than your body, your thoughts, and your circumstances. You are a spiritual being on a unique human journey. Your capacity for growth, transformation, and transcendence is limitless.

These words are not absolute truths but guideposts on your path. Your journey toward spiritual sight is deeply personal. I encourage you to read with an open heart and a curious mind. Ask questions, contemplate, and try the practices. Trust your intuition, your inner guide on this adventure.

Together, we embark on a transformational journey. This book holds the wisdom you need to open your third eye and glimpse the wondrous tapestry of existence.

May this book be your guiding light as you walk the path toward spiritual sight. May it empower you to realize the boundless potential within. Remember, you're not alone. Many souls are awakening to their spiritual sight, and together, we co-create a world filled with love, compassion, and understanding.

With gratitude and excitement for the journey ahead,

Joseph Manuel Garcia

CHAPTER 1

Seeing is Believing

In a world where everyone possesses unique gifts and talents, people are naturally drawn to one another based on their abilities. Whether it's the mesmerizing melodies of musicians, the captivating voices of singers, the awe-inspiring artwork created by artists, or even the mental strength of an athlete, these creative talents profoundly impact our emotions.

Not only do artistic talents move us, but we are also captivated by athletes who possess incredible physical abilities and businesspeople with a remarkable knack for creating and growing successful ventures. Teachers, too, have the gift of inspiring others to learn and explore subjects they are passionate about.

What lies beneath these talents and skills is the expression of one's higher self. Some may even say these remarkable abilities manifest God's love through individuals. We are intrigued and attracted when we witness someone wholeheartedly pursuing their passion and honing their skills. On a subconscious level, we hope such individuals will dedicate the same level of attention and love to their spirituality.

Feeling seen and understood by others is another aspect that touches our hearts. When someone notices the subtleties about us and compliments us on them, we experience a sense of closeness and connection. Similarly, God, who sees even the most concealed aspects of ourselves, including our flaws and weaknesses, desires us to develop and transform those areas. When we seek to overcome our shortcomings and strive for growth, God sheds light on our imperfections, revealing where we've gone astray for betterment or evolution.

This is where spiritual sight comes into play. As souls residing in physical bodies, our ultimate quest is to purify ourselves and allow the divine within us to shine. The ability to see one's spirit, all spirits, auras, and all within the spiritual realm for all things of matter have a spiritual counterpart and can be manifested to a level of degree. You can only progress in life so much with the thought of physicality alone. There is the mentality of life for life and the spirituality of and for life, and it is advantageous to see and interact with such. Unfortunately, the challenges of daily life often distract us, leading to a diminished expression of our true selves. City driving, work stress, relationship issues, and various personal struggles weigh us down, preventing the growth of our spiritual side. We have not been taught how to nurture our spiritual selves.

We associate spirituality with activities that bring us peace, inspiration, and wisdom. However, true spirituality is rooted in love, Passion, and curiosity. The foundations of spiritual belief are learning how to love, be respectful, and keep our hearts open despite pain.

As individuals embark on their spiritual journeys and cultivate sight within themselves, a remarkable transformation occurs—their spiritual sight awakens. By reducing reliance on stimulants, embracing healthier lifestyles, and balancing their masculine and feminine aspects, their awareness of the world expands.

Spiritual sight goes beyond physical vision. It is the ability to perceive the unseen—energetic aspects, patterns, blocks, and expressions of God. Spiritual teachers often refer to this expanded awareness as "Christ Consciousness," a state of being receptive to what truly exists beneath the surface. I consider this a spiritual sight and a strong mind. It allows individuals to understand themselves, others, and the world more deeply.

Spiritual sight is an essential tool for those called to be spiritual guides, such as priests. People seek their counsel to gain an understanding of the profound truths that lie beyond their own perception. However, being a proper guide means approaching each situation with love and empathy rather than simply adhering to strict doctrines. It requires tuning into the underlying energies, listening attentively, and discerning what is best for the person seeking guidance.

Developing spiritual sight requires a proactive and disciplined approach. It begins with establishing a relationship with God and seeking guidance from oneself who can help identify areas where personal growth is needed. Self-purification is also crucial, involving reducing negative influences, respecting and caring for the body, and practicing meditation, devotion, and service work. Through these efforts, the light within oneself intensifies, allowing for a profound shift in perspective, for your body is your temple, your spirituality is your service, and your mind is your life.

In a world rife with darkness and confusion, individuals who develop their spiritual sight become beacons of hope, shining light on the paths of others. They perceive life from a spiritual perspective, recognizing the interconnectedness of all beings and the boundless love that underlies our existence. Through their transformation, they inspire and guide others to embark on their spiritual journeys, embracing their unique gifts and becoming agents of positive change in the world. Individuals who develop their spiritual sight become beacons of hope, shining light on the paths of others. They perceive life from a spiritual perspective, recognizing the interconnectedness of all beings and the boundless love that underlies our existence. Through their transformation, they inspire and guide others to embark on their spiritual journeys, embracing their unique gifts and becoming agents of positive change in the world. As these spiritual guides walk their chosen path, they encounter diverse souls seeking solace, answers, and a deeper understanding of life. Some are burdened by grief, others by confusion, while some are simply yearning for purpose and meaning. With their heightened perception, the spiritual guides see beyond the surface and delve into the essence of each person they encounter. Their spiritual sight enables them to understand the root causes of suffering and offer guidance that resonates with the deepest parts of the individual's being. They listen attentively, their hearts filled with compassion and love, providing a safe space for others to express their fears, doubts, and vulnerabilities. The spiritual guides recognize that each person's journey is unique and honor the diversity of experiences and beliefs. They do not impose their views but act as channels for divine wisdom and guidance. Their role is to facilitate the growth and transformation of those they serve, helping them tap into their spiritual sight. Through their presence and teachings, the spiritual guides encourage others to look within themselves, explore their inner landscapes, and connect with the divine essence that resides within. They remind them that the answers they seek lie not outside but deep within their minds. As individuals embark on this inner exploration, their spiritual sight gradually awakens. They begin to perceive the subtle energies that permeate all of creation, sensing the ebb and flow of life's interconnectedness. They develop an intuitive understanding of the underlying patterns and synchronicities that shape their experiences. With this newfound perception, individuals gain clarity in their decision-making, relationships, and life's purpose. They become more attuned to their intuition and the whispers of divine guidance constantly surrounding them. The illusions and distractions of the world lose their grip as they navigate life guided by a higher wisdom.

Although it is not necessary to seek a spiritual guide alone if you are curious, you can become your guide, and the answers and development you seek can come through friends, family, and individual studies. Yet, the path of spiritual sight has its challenges. The awakening of spiritual vision brings with it a heightened sensitivity to the pain and suffering that exists in the world, and you must be strong-willed and minded not to waiver of these. Individuals become acutely aware of societal imbalance, injustice, and disharmony. This newfound awareness compels them to take action to become catalysts for positive change. They use their spiritual sight to understand, heal, and transform. They advocate for justice, equality, and compassion, working towards creating a more harmonious and loving world for all beings. In their journey, these spiritual guides and seekers of spiritual sight understand that the ultimate goal is personal transformation and the upliftment of humanity as a whole. They recognize that the collective awakening of spiritual sight is crucial for the evolution and survival of our planet. As more individuals open themselves to the realms beyond the physical, embracing their spiritual sight and connecting with their divine essence, a profound shift occurs. Love becomes the guiding force in their lives, and they radiate it outwards, touching the lives of those they encounter, though they try not to feel pressured with such liberation. Once shrouded in darkness, the world begins to illuminate with the brilliance of awakened souls. The barriers that separate us crumble, and a sense of unity and oneness prevails. With spiritual sight as their compass, individuals join hands to co-create a world where love, compassion, understanding, and intelligence are the guiding principles. And so, the journey continues as more souls awaken to their spiritual sight and embark on their quests of self-discovery and spiritual growth. They become part of a growing community of seekers, supporting and uplifting one another.

In this shared journey, individuals learn to cultivate stillness and silence within themselves. Through regular meditation and introspection, which seems like a bombardment when speaking of spirituality but is truly helpful for controlling one's sight and reducing stress, they deepen their connection to the divine and attune themselves to the subtle whispers of the universe. They discover that true wisdom arises not from external sources but from the depths of their being.

As they develop their spiritual sight, they gain a profound understanding of the power of the mind and its transformative potential. Will become their guiding principle, shaping their thoughts, words, and actions. They learn to extend their will to themselves and all beings, fostering compassion, forgiveness, acceptance, and adversity.

With their spiritual sight, they perceive the underlying unity that binds all creation. They recognize the divine spark within every living being, and their interactions are guided by reverence and respect for life's inherent sacredness. Their relationships become vessels of growth and healing, nourished by authenticity, empathy, and unconditional love.

As they navigate the complexities of the modern world, individuals with awakened spiritual sight remain grounded in their spiritual practice. They understand the importance of self-care nurturing their physical, emotional, and mental well-being. They strive for balance in all aspects of life, creating space for joy, playfulness, and creative expression.

These spiritual pioneers also recognize the interconnectedness between their inner world and the external environment. They embrace a lifestyle that honors and protects the Earth, mindful of their impact on nature and future generations. They advocate for sustainable practices, environmental stewardship, and conscious consumption.

In their continued pursuit of spiritual growth, individuals with awakened spiritual sight recognize that they are forever students, constantly learning, evolving, and deepening their understanding. They seek wisdom from ancient traditions, spiritual teachings, and the knowledge of the natural world.

With each step on their spiritual journey, they inspire others to embark on their paths of self-discovery and inner transformation. They become beacons of light, radiating love, wisdom, and compassion to all they encounter. Their presence alone brings comfort, solace, and hope in a world often overshadowed by darkness.

And so, the ripple effect of spiritual sight continues, expanding and touching lives far beyond what the eye can see. It is a journey of awakening, remembering our true essence, and rediscovering the interconnectedness of all existence.

As more individuals embrace their spiritual sight, humanity's collective consciousness evolves, fostering unity, harmony, and love. This is a profound shift, a new era where the spiritual and the material merge, and humanity walks hand in hand with the divine.

In this awakened state, individuals with spiritual sight recognize that the journey is not just about personal enlightenment but about contributing to the greater good. They become agents of positive change, healers, teachers, and guides for those seeking spiritual awakening.

And so, the story of spiritual sight continues to unfold, inviting us to embark on our own sacred quest, to open our hearts and minds to the infinite possibilities within. It is a journey of deep introspection, boundless love, and limitless growth that can transform ourselves and the world around us. And as the story of spiritual sight unfolds, we witness the emergence of communities dedicated to this shared path of awakening. These communities become sanctuaries of love, wisdom, and support, where individuals gather to nurture their spiritual growth and explore the depths of their souls.

Within these communities, spiritual teachers and guides arise, offering their wisdom and guidance to those who seek it. These mentors have traversed the inner realms, honing their spiritual sight and cultivating a deep connection with the divine. They serve as beacons of inspiration, illuminating the path for others and empowering them to embrace their spiritual gifts.

In the presence of these teachers, individuals undergo profound transformations. They shed layers of conditioning, limiting beliefs and fears, unveiling their true essence. They learn to harness their innate spiritual power and manifest their highest potential through sacred rituals, ceremonies, and teachings.

But the journey of spiritual sight has its challenges. As individuals delve into the depths of their being, they confront their shadows—the aspects of themselves that need healing and transformation. This inner work requires courage, vulnerability, and a willingness to face the darkest corners of their souls.

Yet, with the support of their spiritual community and mentors' guidance, individuals find the strength to confront their shadows head-on. They embrace their imperfections, acknowledging that the journey to spiritual sight is a continuous growth and integration process.

Through this inner alchemy, individuals experience profound healing and liberation. They release old patterns of fear, doubt, and self-limitation, allowing the radiant light of their authentic selves to shine through. They reclaim their power and voice and step into their roles as co-creators of their reality.

Individuals embody their spiritual sight and become catalysts for positive change in the world. Their expanded awareness allows them to recognize and address humanity's social, environmental, and systemic challenges. They become advocates for justice, equality, and sustainability, working towards a more harmonious and compassionate world.

The ripple effects of their actions spread far and wide, touching the lives of countless individuals and communities. Through their love, wisdom, and service, they inspire others to awaken their spiritual sight and join the collective movement toward a more enlightened society.

And so, the story of spiritual sight unfolds, inviting us all to embark on this transformative journey. It is a call to reconnect with our divine essence, embrace our innate gifts and talents, and align our lives with the highest expressions of love and truth.

May we all have the courage to open our hearts and minds, cultivate our spiritual sight, and contribute to co-creating a world filled with compassion, harmony, and deep spiritual connection.

CHAPTER 2
The Awakening

You feel an insatiable longing in the depths of your bustling city amidst the noise and chaos. You yearn for something beyond the ordinary, a deeper meaning to your existence. Walking through the crowded streets, you can't shake the feeling that there is more to life than what meets the eye.

One fateful evening, as the sun dips below the horizon, you find yourself drawn to a small bookstore in a quiet corner. Something about its weathered exterior and flickering lights beckons you inside. As you enter the door, a sense of serenity washes over you, as if the bookstore holds a secret portal to a different realm.

Your eyes scan the shelves adorned with ancient texts, spiritual teachings, and mystical wisdom. One book glows, calling out to you with an invisible force. Its title reads "The Path of Awakening: Unveiling the Mysteries Within."

Curiosity piqued, you reach for the book and delicately open its pages. Words dance before your eyes, illuminating the path you have been yearning for. The book speaks of inner transformation, spiritual sight, and the awakening of the divine within.

With each turn of the page, you feel a fire ignite within your soul. It is as if the words are breathing life into your deepest desires, reminding you of a forgotten truth. This begins a profound journey—an awakening to your spiritual sight.

Eager to explore further, you embark on a quest to seek out spiritual communities, seeking like-minded souls who share your yearning for truth and self-discovery. You attend workshops, retreats, and gatherings, immersing yourself in the wisdom of spiritual teachers and embracing the practices that will unlock your dormant potential.

In the sacred space of these communities, you find solace and support. You meet kindred spirits who have embarked on their paths of awakening. Together, you delve into meditation, energy healing, and ancient rituals, peeling away the layers of conditioning and stepping into the expansive realm of spiritual sight.

Under the guidance of wise mentors, you learn to quiet your mind and listen to the whispers of your intuition. You discover the power of your breath, the energy that flows through your body, and the interconnectedness of all things. You experience moments of profound clarity, where you can perceive the subtle energetic patterns and divine essence that permeate every aspect of existence.

As your spiritual sight awakens, your perception of the world transforms. You begin to see beauty and divinity in the ordinary—a flower blooming on a city sidewalk, a stranger's smile, and the symphony of nature's harmonies. You recognize the interconnectedness of all beings and feel a deep sense of compassion and love for humanity.

With your newfound sight, you also become aware of the shadows that veil the world. You see the injustices, the suffering, and the imbalance that exists in society. This awareness ignites a fierce determination within you—a call to be a force of change, to use your spiritual gifts and sight to make a positive impact.

Your journey is challenging. You face moments of doubt and uncertainty when the world's weight feels overwhelming.

But in those moments, you turn inward, drawing strength from the wellspring of divine wisdom within you.

As you deepen your spiritual sight, you discover that true sight is not merely about perceiving the unseen but about embodying love, compassion, and authenticity in every aspect of your life. You learn that spiritual sight is not an isolated gift reserved for a select few but a birthright of every soul longing to remember their divine essence.

And so, your journey of awakening and spiritual sight continues, intertwining with the stories of countless others seeking truth and purpose. Together, you weave a tapestry of transformation as your collective awakening ripples through the world, inspiring others to reclaim their spiritual sight and create a more compassionate, harmonious, and enlightened existence.

In the chapters that lie ahead, you will uncover the hidden depths within yourself, unlocking the wisdom in your heart. The journey may be challenging sometimes, but remember, reader, you are not alone. The universe conspires to guide and support you every step of the way.

Embrace the path of awakening, for it is a path of profound self-discovery, expansion, and the realization of your infinite potential. As you turn the pages of your story, may you find the courage to embrace your spiritual sight and shine your light brightly upon the world.

A dormant power awaits in the depths of your being, ready to awaken and illuminate your path. It is the gift of spiritual sight, a sacred vision that transcends the limitations of the physical senses. As you delve deeper into your spiritual journey, this inner sight becomes a guiding light, revealing profound truths and unveiling the hidden realms of existence.

You realize that the journey to develop your spiritual sight begins within yourself. It is a process of self-discovery and self-transformation. You seek to purify your being, shedding the layers of conditioning and egoic attachments that obscure your inner vision. Through conscious awareness and inner reflection, you become attuned to the subtle energies that flow through your being, discerning the patterns and blocks that hinder your growth.

Cultivating spiritual sight requires a conscious choice to embrace love as the guiding force in your life. You recognize that love is the essence of spirituality; to truly see, you must learn to love unconditionally. You practice the art of giving, making selfless sacrifices for the benefit of others. In the face of negativity and adversity, you choose not to react but to respond with an open heart, emanating love even amid pain.

As you deepen your commitment to spiritual growth, you notice a transformation within yourself. Your senses become attuned to the subtle expressions of energy that permeate the world around you. You perceive the beauty in the simplest moments, the interconnectedness of all beings, and the divine presence that weaves through every experience.

Expanding your spiritual sight opens your eyes to the deeper truths beyond surface appearances. You begin recognizing the energetic dynamics in your relationships and interactions. With compassion and understanding, you see beyond the masks people wear, perceiving their true essence and the struggles they carry within. Your ability to empathize and connect deepens, fostering a sense of closeness and shared understanding.

Yet, spiritual sight is not solely about perceiving the light. It also involves the courage to confront the shadows within yourself. With unwavering honesty, you acknowledge and transform the aspects of your being that are "off"—the character defects, flaws, and negative tendencies that hinder your spiritual growth. In the presence of divine love, you surrender these aspects, allowing them to be transformed and transmuted.

As your spiritual sight develops, you realize it is not a solitary journey. You seek out teachers and guides who can support and illuminate your path. They help you uncover the blind spots and barriers that hinder your spiritual sight, guiding you toward a deeper understanding of yourself and the world.

Each step forward expands your spiritual sight, revealing a more profound and vibrant reality. You witness the interplay of energies, the dance of light and shadow, and the intricate tapestry of existence. Through the lens of spiritual sight, you perceive the divine presence that flows through all creation, and you are filled with a sense of awe, wonder, and reverence. The concept of the third eye has intrigued not only spiritual seekers but also scientists who have delved into the intricate workings of the human brain. While the third eye is often associated with metaphysical and spiritual experiences, it can also be understood from a more medical standpoint, focusing on the pineal gland, a small endocrine gland located deep within the brain. Here are some insights into the medical approach to opening your third eye and activating your pineal gland:

Deep within the human brain resides the pineal gland, a small, pea-sized structure. It's renowned for its role in producing melatonin, the hormone responsible for regulating our sleep-wake cycles. However, the pineal gland is not a one-trick pony; it's also a key player in the synthesis of dimethyltryptamine (DMT), a compound associated with altered states of consciousness and profound spiritual experiences. (DMT) - is a substance that can make people see strange and colorful things and feel like they're in a dream for a little while. It's naturally found in some plants and animals and can be created by the human mind, but it is something to use only if your brain makes it naturally. Aside from that fact (DMT) is not the reason for your spiritual sight; it is but a tiny part of the ability; the majority of the ability comes from the frontal lobe and pineal gland, and the operation and functionality of said sight and spiritual realm comes from the entire brain specifically for sight prefrontal cortex, medial temporal lobes, posterior cingulate, precuneus. And for meditation, specifically the prefrontal cortex, anterior cingulate cortex, insula, posterior cingulate cortex, hippocampus, amygdala, and thalamus.

To optimize the function of this mysterious gland, we must start with the cornerstone of a good night's sleep. Your bedroom becomes the stage for this critical performance. It should be a haven of darkness, silence, and solitude, free from disturbances. Establishing a consistent bedtime routine, including relaxation practices like meditation or gentle yoga, sets the scene for deep and restorative sleep, ultimately supporting the optimal performance of the pineal gland.

Sunlight is the next character in our story, as it significantly influences the pineal gland. Embrace the outdoors during daylight hours to bask in natural light. This exposure stimulates the pineal gland and helps it synchronize with your daily rhythms. Walking, gardening, or simply soaking up the sun's warmth can awaken the pineal gland's functions.

Mindfulness plays a vital role as well. Be conscious of what you consume, for certain substances can affect the pineal gland. Steer clear of processed foods, artificial additives, caffeine, and alcohol. Instead, prioritize a well-balanced diet rich in whole foods, antioxidants, and brain-nourishing nutrients.

Now, let's confront a formidable opponent – fluoride. This adversary is often found in tap water and oral hygiene products, infiltrating the pineal gland and potentially hindering its function. To thwart this threat, opt for fluoride-free water for drinking and cooking. Seek natural alternatives for oral care. Additionally, support your body's natural detoxification processes through exercise, hydration, and a diet that includes detoxifying foods.

Meditation takes center stage in our journey. Regular practice, especially visualization techniques, can stir the pineal gland from slumber. Envision a radiant, vibrant light at the center of your forehead, symbolizing the opening and activation of your third eye. This visualization fosters a deep connection between your mind and body, facilitating the alignment and functioning of the pineal gland.

For those seeking an extra boost, consider dietary supplements like melatonin. But remember to consult with a healthcare professional before adding supplements to your routine, as they may interact with medications or have individual considerations.

In conclusion, it's vital to acknowledge that the medical perspective on the third eye, often associated with the pineal gland, is still a subject of ongoing research. Individual experiences vary in this intricate journey, exploring the relationship between brain chemistry, consciousness, and spiritual encounters.

As our story draws to a close, let us remember the wisdom of a holistic approach to well-being. Nurture your body, mind, and spirit to support the optimal functioning of your pineal gland and the awakening of your third eye. May your quest to understand the pineal gland be a remarkable journey filled with self-discovery, growth, and enlightenment.

CHAPTER 3

Your Pineal Gland

Within your being lies a dormant power waiting to be awakened—the ability to perceive beyond the physical realm and tap into higher states of consciousness. In this chapter, we explore the path to activating your spiritual sight, delving into the mystical realm of the pineal gland and its connection to expanded perception.

The pineal gland, often associated with the third eye, is a remarkable structure deep within your brain. Scientifically known as the pineal body, this tiny gland has long been revered for its mystical qualities and potential to open doors to spiritual realms. Understanding the pineal gland's role in perception is the key to unlocking your inner vision.

To embark on this transformative journey, creating an environment that nurtures your spiritual growth is essential. Begin by carving out sacred space—a sanctuary within your home where you can retreat and focus on your inner self.

Fill this space with objects that resonate with your spiritual aspirations—crystals, sacred symbols, or meaningful artifacts. Make it a sanctuary of peace and tranquility where you can connect with your deepest essence.

Meditation becomes an invaluable tool in your pursuit of activating your spiritual sight. Through regular practice, you can calm the mind's constant chatter and cultivate a state of inner stillness. Find a comfortable position, close your eyes, and take deep, mindful breaths. As you sink into a meditative state, turn your attention to the center of your forehead—the location of the third eye.

Visualize a radiant and vibrant light emanating from this point, gradually expanding and enveloping your entire being. Feel the warmth and energy of this light permeating every cell of your body, awakening your spiritual senses. Allow yourself to connect with the subtle energies beyond the physical realm, opening the gateway to heightened perception.

In addition to meditation, the pineal gland responds to the power of intention and focused thought. Develop a daily ritual of setting clear intentions for your spiritual growth and activating your third eye. Write down your intentions in a journal or speak them aloud, infusing them with conviction and belief. As you do so, imagine your intentions as tangible manifestations already in reality.

Just as the pineal gland is sensitive to light, it is equally influenced by darkness. Establishing a healthy sleep routine is crucial for nurturing your spiritual sight. Create a peaceful, soothing sleep environment free from distractions and electronic devices. Prioritize quality sleep by ensuring you get sufficient rest each night. As you sleep, the pineal gland secretes melatonin, supporting your body's natural rhythms and facilitating spiritual experiences.

Remember that your physical well-being is interconnected with your spiritual growth. Nourish your body with wholesome, natural foods that promote optimal brain function. Emphasize a diet rich in fruits, vegetables, and whole grains while minimizing processed foods and artificial additives. Hydrate your body adequately, as water plays a vital role in the overall health of your pineal gland.

To activate your spiritual sight, be mindful of substances inhibiting the pineal gland's function. Reduce your consumption of stimulants like caffeine and alcohol, as they can disrupt your body's natural balance. Opt for herbal teas and nourishing elixirs, such as chamomile or passionflower tea, that support the well-being of your pineal gland.

It is also essential to clean your body and mind from toxins that accumulate over time. Engage in regular physical exercise to promote circulation and detoxification. Explore holistic practices like yoga or qigong, which harmonize the body and mind, clearing stagnant energy and revitalizing your spiritual senses.

As you embark on activating your spiritual sight, be patient with yourself. Remember that this is a profoundly personal journey, and each individual's experience is unique. Trust in the process, and allow your inner wisdom to guide you. With dedication, practice, and an open heart, you will gradually unlock the profound gifts of your spiritual sight, unveiling a world of limitless possibilities and profound connection with the divine.

Explore various techniques and practices to enhance your journey towards activating your spiritual sight. Consider incorporating the following into your daily routine:

Mindful Observation: Cultivate a heightened sense of awareness in your everyday life. Pay attention to the details of your surroundings, noticing colors, textures, and energy vibrations. Engage all your senses fully, allowing yourself to experience the present moment truly.

Energy Work: Explore modalities such as Reiki, acupuncture, or sound healing to balance and harmonize the energy centers within your body. These practices can help remove energetic blockages and promote the flow of vital energy, supporting the activation of your spiritual sight.

Dream Journaling: Keep a journal by your bedside to record your dreams upon waking. Dreams can be a gateway to the subconscious and offer valuable insights and symbolic messages. By recalling and analyzing your dreams, you may uncover hidden aspects of yourself and receive guidance for your spiritual journey.

Sacred Geometry and Symbols: Explore the profound power of sacred geometry and symbols in awakening your spiritual sight. Meditate upon sacred geometric shapes such as the Flower of Life or visualize spiritual symbols that resonate with you. These visual tools can help attune your consciousness to higher frequencies and expand your perception.

Sound and Vibrational Healing: Experiment with sound therapy, whether through chanting, singing bowls, or guided meditation with binaural beats. Sound vibrations have the potential to activate and awaken dormant aspects of your consciousness, facilitating a deeper connection to your spiritual sight.

Nature Connection: Spend time in nature regularly, immersing yourself in its beauty and tranquility. Nature has a way of grounding and aligning our energies, opening up channels of perception. Take walks in the forest, sit by the ocean, or find solace in a peaceful garden. As you connect with the natural world, allow its wisdom and healing energies to nourish your spiritual sight.

Remember, activating your spiritual sight is an ongoing process of self-discovery and growth. It requires patience, perseverance, and an open mind. Embrace each experience, whether subtle or profound, as a stepping stone on your path. Trust in your innate ability to awaken and expand your spiritual vision and embrace the profound transformations that await you.

The third eye, often referred to as the "pineal gland," is a concept with roots in various spiritual and esoteric traditions. It is believed to be an energetic center or a metaphysical "eye" located in the middle of the forehead, just above the space between the eyebrows.

The pineal gland has been associated with spiritual perception, intuition, and inner vision in many ancient cultures and spiritual systems. This association stems from its anatomical location and role in producing certain biochemical substances that can influence consciousness.

Scientifically, the pineal gland is a small endocrine gland located deep within the brain in a region called the epithalamus. It is about the size of a pea and is shaped like a pinecone, hence the name "pineal gland." The gland's primary function is the production of melatonin, a hormone that regulates sleep and wakefulness and helps maintain the body's circadian rhythm.

However, the pineal gland is also known to produce other substances, including dimethyltryptamine (DMT), a naturally occurring psychedelic compound. DMT is believed to play a role in altered states of consciousness, mystical experiences, and spiritual awakening. Some people associate the activation of the third eye with an increased production or release of DMT within the pineal gland.

In metaphysical and spiritual traditions, the third eye is considered the seat of inner vision and spiritual insight. It is often associated with concepts such as clairvoyance, psychic abilities, and the ability to perceive subtle energies and dimensions beyond the physical realm. Opening or activating the third eye is believed to enable individuals to access higher states of consciousness, expand their perception, and gain deeper insights into themselves and the world around them. To open the pineal gland, imagine the middle of your eyebrows moving forward, a flower bulb opening or even an eye trying to open all just barely above the middle of your eyebrows. It is really that simple; it's a lot of training to have control over it.

As mentioned earlier, various practices are believed to support the activation of the third eye and the development of spiritual sight. These practices aim to balance and harmonize the energy centers within the body, clear blockages, and cultivate a heightened sense of awareness and intuition.

It's important to note that while the concept of the third eye and its association with the pineal gland has spiritual and esoteric significance, scientific research on this topic is still ongoing. The exact role and function of the pineal gland in spiritual experiences and consciousness expansion are still subjects of exploration and debate within the scientific community. In our exploration of spiritual sight and the awakening of the third eye, one aspect that holds excellent fascination is clairvoyance. Clairvoyance, derived from the French words "Clair" (clear) and "voyance" (vision), refers to the ability to perceive information or images beyond the scope of ordinary sensory perception.

Often considered a form of spiritual sight, clairvoyance allows individuals to access knowledge, insights, and visions that extend beyond the physical realm. It is an intuitive ability to see energetic patterns, symbols, colors, and even glimpses of future events.

Clairvoyance can manifest in various ways, and individuals may experience it differently. Some may see vivid images or scenes in their mind's eye, while others may receive flashes of intuition or inner knowing. It is a deeply personal and unique gift that can be nurtured and developed through practice.

To embark on the path of clairvoyance, it is essential to cultivate certain qualities and engage in specific practices. Here are some key elements to consider:

Openness and Receptivity: Developing clairvoyance requires an open mind and a willingness to receive information beyond the limitations of the physical senses. Cultivate a sense of curiosity, wonder, and trust in your intuitive abilities.

Meditation and Visualization: Regular meditation practice enhances concentration, focus, and inner stillness, which are essential for accessing clairvoyant abilities. Visualizations and guided imagery exercises can activate and strengthen your inner vision.

Symbolic Interpretation: Pay attention to the symbols and images in your dreams, visions, and everyday life. Develop the skill of interpreting symbols, as they often carry more profound meanings and insights.

Energy Awareness: Sensitize yourself to subtle energy fields and vibrations. Practice grounding techniques energy-clearing exercises, and work with tools like crystals or color visualization to heighten your sensitivity to energetic frequencies.

Intuition Development: Strengthen your overall intuitive abilities through intuition journaling, card readings, or simply trusting and acting upon your gut feelings. The more you trust your intuition, the more it expands and guides you in developing clairvoyance.

Ethical Considerations: As you explore clairvoyance, it is vital to approach it with integrity and ethical considerations. Use your clairvoyant abilities for the highest good, respecting the privacy and consent of others and maintaining personal boundaries.

Seek Guidance and Support: Connect with like-minded individuals, mentors, or spiritual communities who can offer guidance and support on your clairvoyant journey. Sharing experiences, learning from others, and receiving feedback can be immensely helpful in developing your abilities.

Remember, clairvoyance is a skill that can be honed with practice and dedication. Each person's clairvoyant abilities may unfold at a different pace and in unique ways. Embrace your journey with patience, self-compassion, and a sense of adventure as you explore the realms of clairvoyance and expand your spiritual sight.

In the forthcoming chapters, we will explore practical exercises, techniques, and insights to deepen your clairvoyant abilities and enhance your spiritual connection. Together, we will navigate the realms of intuition, symbolism, and energetic perception, unraveling the mysteries of clairvoyance and awakening the true potential of your spiritual sight.

Clairvoyance is the ability to perceive or gain information about objects, people, events, or situations through extrasensory perception (ESP) or "the sixth sense." It is frequently associated with spiritual sight, as it involves gaining insights and information beyond the scope of ordinary sensory perception.

In its essence, clairvoyance is the ability to "see clearly" or "see beyond" the physical realm. It goes beyond the limitations of the five physical senses (sight, hearing, touch, taste, and smell) and allows individuals to access information intuitively or psychically. Clairvoyants may receive information in images, symbols, visions, or impressions that are not perceived through normal visual perception.

Clairvoyance is often considered a natural extension of the third eye or the spiritual sight. It is believed to involve the activation of the intuitive faculties and the ability to tap into higher levels of consciousness. Those who possess clairvoyant skills may be able to perceive energies, auras, or subtle vibrations associated with people, places, or objects. They may also receive insights or glimpses into the past, present, or future.

It's important to note that clairvoyance is not limited to seeing with the physical eyes or predicting future events. It can also involve inner vision or the ability to "see" and understand abstract concepts, spiritual truths, or energetic patterns. Clairvoyance can encompass various forms of perception, such as clairaudience (hearing), clairsentience (feeling), or claircognizance (knowing).

Developing clairvoyance and spiritual sight often requires practice, awareness, and the cultivation of one's intuitive abilities. Meditation, energy work, and other spiritual practices can help individuals enhance their clairvoyant abilities by clearing energetic blockages, expanding their awareness, and strengthening their connection to higher realms of consciousness.

It's vital to approach clairvoyance and spiritual sight with an open mind and discernment. Not all experiences or information received through clairvoyant means may be accurate or relevant to an individual's spiritual growth. Developing a sense of discernment and grounding oneself in personal ethics and spiritual principles can help maintain a balanced and responsible approach to clairvoyant experiences.

With this understanding of clairvoyance and its connection to spiritual sight, we can explore further aspects of spiritual awakening and the expansion of consciousness in the upcoming chapters. As we delve deeper into the realms of spiritual sight and expanded consciousness, one aspect that holds immense significance is the awakening of the third eye. Often referred to as the seat of intuition and spiritual vision, the third eye is closely associated with the pineal gland.

The pineal gland, a small pea-sized gland located in the center of the brain, has been regarded by various spiritual traditions as the physical counterpart to the third eye. It is believed to be pivotal in facilitating spiritual experiences and opening the doorway to higher states of consciousness.

In many ancient cultures, the third eye, symbolized by an eye-shaped object, represents an intuitive and inner vision that goes beyond physical sight. It is often depicted as a metaphorical eye located between the eyebrows, corresponding to the anatomical position of the pineal gland.

While the third eye is often considered dormant or inactive in most individuals, it has the potential to be awakened and developed through various practices and techniques. The awakening of the third eye can lead to heightened intuition, expanded awareness, and a deeper connection to the spiritual dimensions.

So, how can one awaken the third eye and unlock its potential? Here are some approaches that can be explored:

Meditation is a fundamental practice for opening the third eye. By quieting the mind and focusing inward, meditation cultivates inner stillness and heightened awareness. Specific meditation techniques, such as focusing on the area between the eyebrows or visualizing an inner light, can help activate the third eye and facilitate its awakening.

Energy Work: Working with the body's subtle energy systems, such as the chakras and meridians, can support the awakening of the third eye. Practices like Reiki, pranayama (breathwork), and Qigong can help balance and activate the energy centers, including the third eye, promoting greater energetic flow and spiritual receptivity.

Intuitive Development: Engaging in activities that enhance your intuitive abilities can also contribute to awakening the third eye. This may involve practicing divination methods like tarot reading or pendulum dowsing, journaling to tap into your inner guidance, or simply trusting and following your intuition in daily life.

Sacred Rituals and Ceremonies: Participating in holy rituals or ceremonies that honor and invoke spiritual energies can create a conducive environment for awakening the third eye. These rituals may involve using crystals, incense, sacred chants, or specific rituals from various spiritual traditions.

Lifestyle Adjustments: Making conscious lifestyle choices can also support the awakening of the third eye. This includes adopting a healthy diet, reducing exposure to toxins, spending time in nature, and nurturing a sense of inner balance and harmony.

Remember, awakening the third eye is a personal and unique journey for each individual. It requires patience, practice, and an open mind. It is essential to approach this process with respect, integrity, and a willingness to explore your inner self.

As we progress through this transformative journey of awakening the third eye, we will delve deeper into the profound experiences, insights, and spiritual growth that accompany the expansion of our spiritual sight. In the following chapters, we will explore practical exercises, guidance, and wisdom to support you on your path of spiritual awakening and the discovery of your inner vision.

The inner realms are the vast landscapes of consciousness, accessible through our awakened third eye and developed clairvoyant abilities. These realms are not bound by the constraints of time and space, offering a space of infinite possibilities, wisdom, and guidance.

Here are some of the inner realms that clairvoyants often traverse:

The Astral Plane: The astral plane is a realm of subtle energy and vibrations parallel to the physical world. It is a dimension where dreams, visions, and astral travel occur. In this realm, clairvoyants can encounter spirit guides and deceased loved ones and explore different energetic frequencies.

The Akashic Records: The Akashic Records, often called the "Book of Life," is believed to be a vast, energetic library that contains the collective knowledge and experiences of all souls throughout time. Clairvoyants can access this realm to gain insights, wisdom, and information about past lives, soul contracts, and the soul's journey.

Spirit Realms: The spirit realms encompass various dimensions where spirit beings reside. These realms include angelic realms, nature spirit realms, and realms inhabited by higher-dimensional beings. Clairvoyants can connect with these realms to communicate with spirit guides, receive guidance, and tap into higher wisdom.

Symbolic Realms: Symbolism plays a significant role in clairvoyant perception. Symbolic realms are multidimensional spaces where symbols and archetypes exist in their purest form. Exploring these realms allows clairvoyants to unlock deeper meanings, receive profound insights, and access collective unconscious information.

Healing Realms: The inner realms also hold spaces dedicated to healing and transformation. These realms are infused with potent energies and healing vibrations that can assist in physical, emotional, and spiritual healing.

Clairvoyants can work with these realms to facilitate energy healing, soul retrieval, and personal growth.

You will gradually gain access to these inner realms as you develop your clairvoyant abilities and open your spiritual sight. Remember that each individual's experiences may vary, and exploring the inner realms is a highly personal journey.

In the upcoming chapters, we will explore specific techniques and exercises for navigating and exploring these realms. We will learn how to establish energetic boundaries, strengthen our connection with spirit guides, interpret symbolic messages, and harness the transformative power of the inner realms.

Prepare yourself for a captivating expedition as we embark on a quest to unravel the mysteries and embrace the profound wisdom that awaits within the inner realms. Prepare to expand your spiritual sight and discover the limitless possibilities beyond the physical world. In the following few chapters, I'll tell you more about how to care for and improve your overall spiritual sight.

CHAPTER 4

Optimize Sleep

Sleep is a fundamental pillar of our overall well-being and plays a crucial role in the proper functioning of the pineal gland. The pineal gland in the brain's center produces melatonin, a hormone that regulates sleep and wakefulness. However, the pineal gland's role extends beyond melatonin production, as it is also involved in other vital functions related to our physical and mental health.

Creating a sleep-friendly environment is essential to supporting the optimal functioning of the pineal gland. Start by ensuring your bedroom provides the ideal conditions for restful sleep. Keep the room dark, as exposure to light, especially the incredibly blue light emitted by electronic devices, can suppress melatonin production and disrupt your sleep-wake cycle. Use blackout curtains, shades, or an eye mask to block out unwanted light sources.

In addition to darkness, prioritize a quiet sleep environment. Noise disturbances can disrupt sleep quality and interfere with the pineal gland's ability to regulate melatonin secretion effectively. Use earplugs, a white noise machine, or soundproofing techniques to minimize external noises and create a tranquil atmosphere conducive to deep sleep.

Distractions can also hinder the pineal gland's functioning and disrupt sleep. Remove electronic devices, such as smartphones or tablets, from your bedroom to minimize the temptation to use them before bed. Instead, establish a "technology-free zone" and create a peaceful sanctuary that promotes relaxation and restfulness.

Consistency is vital when it comes to sleep. Establish a regular sleep schedule by going to bed and waking up at the same time each day, even on weekends. This helps regulate your body's internal clock and promotes a more balanced secretion of hormones, including melatonin. By aligning your sleep schedule with your natural circadian rhythm, you support the optimal functioning of the pineal gland and enhance your overall sleep quality.

Prioritizing relaxation before bed is another crucial aspect of optimizing sleep and supporting the pineal gland. Engage in calming activities that promote a sense of tranquility and prepare your mind and body for sleep. Practices such as meditation, deep breathing exercises, or gentle yoga can help induce relaxation, reduce stress levels, and enhance your ability to fall asleep quickly.

It's worth noting that the pineal gland is susceptible to environmental cues, especially light exposure. During the day, expose yourself to natural sunlight, particularly in the morning, as it helps regulate your internal clock and melatonin production. Spend time outdoors, walk, or open the curtains to let natural light into your living space. This exposure to natural light during the day can positively impact your sleep quality and overall well-being.

By nurturing a healthy sleep routine and optimizing your sleep environment, you create optimal conditions for the pineal gland to function optimally. Adequate and restful sleep allows for the proper secretion of melatonin, ensuring a well-regulated sleep-wake cycle and supporting various physiological and psychological processes in the body.

Remember, a balanced and healthy lifestyle encompasses good nutrition and exercise and prioritizes the quality of sleep. By optimizing sleep, you provide the pineal gland with the necessary support to perform its functions effectively, promoting overall well-being and vitality.

Dreams, daydreams, and thought projection hold a profound connection to spiritual sight. These phenomena provide gateways to the deeper layers of our consciousness, allowing us to explore the realms beyond the physical and tap into our innate spiritual abilities. In this chapter, we will delve into the significance of dreaming, daydreaming, and thought projection in relation to spiritual sight.

Dreams have been revered throughout history as powerful vehicles for spiritual insight and communication with higher realms. During sleep, our conscious mind rests while our subconscious mind becomes more active. This opens the doorway to profound experiences, symbolism, and messages from our inner selves, guides, or even the divine. We can unravel hidden truths, receive guidance, and expand our spiritual awareness by paying attention to the symbols, emotions, and narratives within our dreams.

Daydreaming: Daydreaming, often considered a form of spontaneous, imaginative thinking, allows us to tap into the creative and intuitive aspects of our mind. It bridges the conscious and subconscious realms, offering opportunities for exploration, visualization, and manifestation. Daydreaming can be consciously directed, where we intentionally enter a state of focused imagination, or occur naturally as our mind wanders. By harnessing the power of daydreaming, we can engage in active visualization, affirmations, and intention setting, amplifying our spiritual sight and aligning with our desires.

Thought Projection: Thought projection, also known as mental projection or remote viewing, is the ability to extend one's consciousness beyond the physical body to perceive distant locations, events, or information. Individuals can tap into their spiritual sight to access non-local information or experiences through focused intention, deep concentration, and heightened awareness. Thought projection allows us to transcend the limitations of space and time, opening doors to profound insights, remote healing, and connections with higher dimensions.

By recognizing the significance of dreams, daydreams, and thought projection, we can consciously cultivate and harness these experiences to enhance our spiritual sight. Practicing techniques such as dream journaling, lucid dreaming, intentional daydreaming, and remote viewing exercises can expand our awareness, sharpen our intuitive abilities, and provide a deeper understanding of ourselves and the interconnected nature of existence.

Dreams have long captivated human curiosity, offering a window into our subconscious mind and providing a glimpse into hidden realms of our psyche. Understanding the role of REM sleep and learning how to enhance your dream awareness can deepen your spiritual journey and unlock profound insights. In this chapter, we will delve into the mysteries of REM sleep and explore techniques to optimize your dream experiences.

The Role of REM Sleep: Rapid Eye Movement (REM) sleep is a stage of sleep characterized by vivid dreaming, heightened brain activity, and rapid eye movements. During REM sleep, the pineal gland is particularly active, releasing melatonin and potentially other compounds that influence dream formation. REM sleep is essential for overall cognitive function, emotional well-being, and memory consolidation.

Tips for Enhancing REM Sleep:

a. Maintain a Consistent Sleep Schedule: Establish a regular sleep routine by going to bed and waking up at the same time every day. Consistency helps regulate your body's internal clock and promotes healthy REM sleep patterns.

b. Create a Relaxing Sleep Environment: Make your bedroom a sleep sanctuary. Ensure it is dark, quiet, and free from distractions. Use comfortable bedding, regulate the temperature, and consider using white noise machines or earplugs to create a peaceful atmosphere conducive to REM sleep.

c. Reduce Stimulants and Electronics: Avoid consuming stimulants like caffeine and nicotine close to bedtime, as they can interfere with REM sleep. Additionally, limit exposure to electronic devices before sleep, as the blue light emitted by screens can disrupt your natural sleep-wake cycle.

d. Incorporate Relaxation Techniques: Before bed, engage in relaxation techniques such as meditation, deep breathing exercises, or gentle stretching. These practices can help calm your mind and prepare your body for rest, promoting more vivid dreams during REM sleep.

e. Keep a Dream Journal: Keep a notebook and pen by your bedside to record your dreams immediately upon waking. By capturing the details of your dreams, you train your mind to become more aware of the dream state and encourage a deeper connection to your subconscious mind.

f. Practice Lucid Dreaming: Lucid dreaming is the ability to become aware that you are dreaming while still in the dream state. Through various techniques, such as reality checks, visualization exercises, and intention setting before sleep, you can cultivate the ability to recognize and control your dreams, opening up extraordinary opportunities for self-exploration and spiritual growth.

By understanding the significance of REM sleep and incorporating these tips into your sleep routine, you can enhance your dream experiences, tap into the wisdom of your subconscious mind, and embark on profound spiritual journeys within the realm of dreams.

CHAPTER 5
Sunlight and Spiritual Tools

In our journey to open and activate our spiritual sight, it is essential to pay attention to the well-being of our pineal gland. This small yet remarkable gland is deeply influenced by sunlight and the quality of substances we consume. By nurturing the pineal gland through sunlight exposure and mindful consumption, we can optimize its functions and enhance our spiritual sight.

Sunlight Exposure: The pineal gland is highly responsive to light, particularly sunlight. Spending time outdoors during daylight hours allows us to absorb natural light, stimulating the pineal gland and supporting its proper functioning. When sunlight enters our eyes, it triggers a cascade of chemical reactions within the pineal gland, synthesizing and releasing various compounds, including melatonin and serotonin. These neurochemicals regulate our sleep-wake cycles, mood, and overall well-being.

To harness the benefits of sunlight exposure, make it a habit to spend time outdoors each day. Engage in activities such as walking, jogging, gardening, or sitting in a sunny spot. Allow the sunlight to touch your skin and enter your eyes, as this direct exposure helps activate the pineal gland. However, protect your skin from excessive sun exposure by applying sunscreen or wearing protective clothing when necessary. Striking a balance between enjoying the benefits of sunlight and practicing sun safety is essential.

Mindful Consumption: Our substances can significantly impact the pineal gland and its functions. To nurture and support the optimal functioning of the pineal gland, it is crucial to be mindful of what we put into our bodies. Certain substances, such as processed foods, artificial additives, and stimulants like caffeine and alcohol, can interfere with the pineal gland's functions and disrupt our spiritual sight.

Instead, prioritize a balanced and nourishing diet that includes whole, unprocessed foods. Emphasize fresh fruits, vegetables, whole grains, lean proteins, and healthy fats. These nutrient-dense foods provide the necessary vitamins, minerals, and antioxidants that support overall brain health, including the pineal gland. Additionally, stay hydrated by drinking adequate water throughout the day, as proper hydration is vital for the optimal functioning of all bodily systems, including the pineal gland.

By consciously choosing to nourish our bodies with wholesome nutrition and exposing ourselves to natural sunlight, we can create an environment that supports the health and activation of the pineal gland. As the pineal gland thrives, our spiritual sight is heightened, and our connection to the spiritual realms deepens.

As we embark on our quest to awaken our spiritual sight and delve into the mystical realms of consciousness, we discover a treasure trove of tools and gems to aid us in our journey. These sacred instruments serve as gateways to higher dimensions, amplifying our intentions and guiding us toward deeper spiritual insights. Their energetic resonance and profound symbolism open doors within us, unlocking hidden potentials and expanding our connection to the spiritual realm.

Among the most revered tools are crystals and gemstones forged deep within the Earth's embrace. These ancient gems hold the wisdom of the ages, resonating with unique frequencies that align with our spiritual centers. Gaze upon the regal amethyst, its purple hues a doorway to higher consciousness. Feel the pure clarity of the quartz crystal, a conduit for divine guidance. And behold the celestial beauty of lapis lazuli, a stone of wisdom and spiritual insight. Through their companionship, we can activate and balance the third eye chakra, awakening our spiritual sight and delving into the mysteries of the unseen.

Guidance awaits us in the realm of cards, where tarot and oracle decks whisper ancient truths as we shuffle the cards; a sacred dialogue unfolds, bridging the realms of the tangible and the ethereal. Each card holds a story, a symbol, a message waiting to be deciphered. Through the wisdom of the cards, we tap into our intuitive wellspring, gaining clarity, guidance, and profound insights into the labyrinth of our spiritual journey. These cards become mirrors, reflecting the whispers of the divine and igniting the flame of our spiritual sight.

Divination tools dance in our hands, conduits of energy and gateways to hidden knowledge. Pendulums swing with purpose, revealing answers to our inquiries, while dowsing rods guide us to unseen, energetic streams. In their delicate dance, we unravel the tapestry of existence, exploring the subtle threads that connect us to the mysteries beyond. With these tools in our grasp, we develop a sensitivity to the unseen, uncovering the truths that lie beneath the surface and expanding our spiritual sight to encompass realms once hidden.

Ritual objects, imbued with sacred intention, become vessels through which we commune with the divine. We light candles, their flickering flames representing the illumination of our inner being—the fragrant tendrils of incense rise, carrying our prayers and intentions to the celestial realms. Sacred symbols and mandalas draw our focus inward, inviting us to journey into the depths of our spiritual sight. Through these rituals, we establish a holy connection, merging the physical and the spiritual, as we step into a realm where our sight transcends the limitations of the material world.

In the embrace of these spiritual tools and gems, we discover a gateway to our inner realms by embracing these spiritual tools and gems. They are catalysts that awaken our dormant abilities and remind us of our inherent divinity. Yet, we must remember that the true power resides within ourselves. These tools are mirrors, reflecting the eternal flame that burns within our souls.

Through our intention, dedication, and inner work, we unlock the full potential of our spiritual sight, traversing the ethereal landscapes and unearthing the profound truths that lie in wait.

So, dear seeker of the mystical, embrace these tools and gems as companions on your spiritual journey. Let them be your allies and guides as you explore the depths of your being. With an open heart and an awakened spirit, may you witness the unseen, perceive the hidden, and embark on a wondrous adventure into the realms of spiritual sight.

Amethyst is a stone of spiritual protection and higher consciousness known for activating and balancing the third eye chakra.

Quartz Crystal - A powerful amplifier of energy, ideal for enhancing spiritual insights and connecting with higher realms.

Lapis Lazuli - A stone of wisdom and inner vision, often used to stimulate the third eye and expand spiritual awareness.

Tarot Cards - A deck of cards used for divination and gaining insights into personal and spiritual matters.

Oracle Cards - Similar to tarot cards, these decks provide guidance and intuitive messages from the divine.

Pendulum - A weighted object suspended on a string or chain, used for divination and accessing intuitive information.

Dowsing Rods - Tools used to detect energy fields or locate hidden substances, often associated with water divination.

Candles - Used in rituals to represent illumination, transformation, and connection to the divine.

Incense - Fragrant smoke is used in spiritual practices to purify, uplift, and create a sacred atmosphere.

Sacred Symbols and Mandalas - Intricate designs and patterns that serve as focal points for meditation and spiritual contemplation.

These tools and gemstones are not only beautiful but also carry specific energetic properties that can support and enhance spiritual sight. By working with them, individuals can deepen their connection to their intuition, expand their consciousness, and embark on a profound spiritual journey. Remember to choose the ones that resonate with you personally and follow your intuition when working with these sacred tools and gemstones.

Tools and gemstones serve as gateways to unlocking hidden realms and deepening our connection to the divine. These sacred artifacts, infused with ancient wisdom and energy, act as catalysts for expanding our spiritual sight and accessing higher states of consciousness.

When working with these tools, it is essential to understand that they are not mere objects but conduits of energy. They respond to our intentions and vibrations, creating a harmonious synergy between the physical and spiritual realms. Whether we use energy to read, react, or activate these tools, their true power lies in the alignment of our intention, focus, and receptivity.

Take, for example, the utilization of gemstones. Each gemstone possesses unique energetic properties that can resonate with specific chakras or energy centers within our bodies. By placing a gemstone such as amethyst or lapis lazuli on the third eye chakra, we initiate a subtle, energetic exchange. The gemstone acts as a key, unlocking the door to our inner vision, heightening our intuitive abilities, and expanding our spiritual sight. As we attune ourselves to the vibration of the gemstone, we activate its inherent qualities, allowing it to harmonize and balance the energies within us.

Similarly, other spiritual tools such as tarot cards, oracle cards, pendulums, and dowsing rods function as conduits between the spiritual and physical realms. Through focused intention and attunement, these tools allow us to tap into our intuitive abilities and receive guidance from the higher realms. They become extensions of our own spiritual sight, providing insights, clarity, and divine messages that guide us on our spiritual journey.

However, it is essential to remember that spiritual sight does not solely rely on external tools and gemstones. It is an innate ability that resides within each of us, waiting to be awakened and cultivated. These tools act as facilitators, assisting us in accessing the deeper layers of our consciousness and expanding our awareness.

The true essence of spiritual sight lies in our connection to the divine, the exploration of our inner landscapes, and the alignment of our mind, body, and spirit. It is through meditation, introspection, and mindful practices that we can quiet the mind, open our hearts, and awaken the dormant potential within us. By nurturing our spiritual growth and embracing the power of these sacred tools, we embark on a transformative journey of self-discovery and enlightenment.

So, let us honor the power of these spiritual tools and gemstones as we embark on a quest to awaken our spiritual sight. May we approach them with reverence, understanding, and an open heart, for they are but gateways to the vast realms of knowledge, wisdom, and divine connection that await us on our spiritual path."

It sounds like myths, but all hold their own truth to their own extent, whether it's picking up energy on an amulet that calls out to you or reading cards; it could even just be using crystals and gems to change one's emotions, spirituals tools, are accurate as I will show you through your sight.

CHAPTER 6
Fluoride and Detoxification

"In our modern world, it is becoming increasingly important to be mindful of the substances we encounter daily, as some of them can have a profound impact on our health and well-being. One such substance is fluoride, which has been a topic of debate due to its potential effects on the pineal gland.

The pineal gland is often referred to as the 'third eye' or the 'seat of the soul'. It plays a vital role in regulating various physiological functions, including sleep patterns and the production of melatonin, a hormone that helps regulate our sleep-wake cycle. However, research suggests that the pineal gland may also be susceptible to the accumulation of fluoride.

Fluoride is commonly found in tap water and oral hygiene products, such as toothpaste and mouthwash. While it has been used for many years to promote dental health and prevent tooth decay, concerns have been raised about its potential impact on overall health, particularly the pineal gland.

Studies have indicated that fluoride can accumulate in the pineal gland over time, forming calcium fluoride crystals. These crystals can potentially impair the functioning of the gland and interfere with its ability to produce melatonin effectively. Melatonin is not only crucial for regulating our sleep-wake cycle but is also associated with other essential processes, including immune function, antioxidant activity, and the regulation of mood and cognition.

If you want to minimize the potential effects of fluoride on the pineal gland, consider using fluoride-free water for drinking and cooking. Many communities now offer fluoride-free water options, or you can explore home water filtration systems that effectively remove fluoride. Additionally, opting for natural oral care alternatives, such as fluoride-free toothpaste and mouthwash, can help reduce fluoride exposure and support the health of your pineal gland.

Furthermore, supporting your body's natural detoxification processes can aid in reducing the buildup of toxins, including fluoride, in the pineal gland. Regular exercise helps stimulate blood circulation and lymphatic flow, promoting the elimination of toxins from the body. Staying hydrated by drinking an adequate amount of water throughout the day also supports detoxification.

Incorporating detoxifying foods into your diet can further assist in eliminating toxins from the body. Fresh fruits and vegetables, notably those rich in antioxidants and fiber, can support the body's natural detoxification pathways. Foods such as leafy greens, cruciferous vegetables, berries, and herbs like cilantro and parsley are known for their detoxifying properties and can aid in reducing the accumulation of toxins in the pineal gland.

By being mindful of fluoride exposure and supporting your body's natural detoxification processes, you can help protect the health and function of your pineal gland. Taking these steps not only promotes overall well-being but also nurtures your spiritual sight and connection to higher realms.

Remember, it is essential to consult with healthcare professionals and conduct thorough research to make informed decisions about your health and well-being. By taking proactive measures to reduce fluoride exposure and support detoxification, you empower yourself to create a healthier environment within your body, allowing your pineal gland to function optimally and fostering a deeper connection to your spiritual sight."

CHAPTER 7

Hz Sound

Sound has long been recognized as a powerful medium that can influence our physical, mental, and spiritual well-being. When it comes to the pineal gland and spiritual sight, specific sound frequencies, often referred to as Hz (hertz), have gained attention for their potential to decalcify the gland and enhance our spiritual perception.

The pineal gland, as previously discussed, plays a crucial role in our spiritual sight and connection to higher realms. However, factors such as fluoride exposure, poor lifestyle choices, and environmental toxins can contribute to the calcification of the pineal gland, potentially obstructing its optimal functioning. This is where specific sound frequencies come into play.

One popular belief is that certain Hz frequencies can stimulate the decalcification process of the pineal gland. These frequencies are often associated with binaural beats, isochronic tones, or specific musical compositions designed to resonate with the pineal gland and stimulate its activity.

The most commonly mentioned frequency for pineal gland decalcification is 432 Hz. Advocates of this frequency claim that it possesses natural healing and transformative properties, helping to break down calcified deposits within the pineal gland and restore its optimal function. It is believed to resonate with the natural harmony and vibrations of the universe, facilitating a deeper connection to one's spiritual self.

Other frequencies often mentioned in relation to pineal gland activation and spiritual sight include 528 Hz (associated with DNA repair and transformation), 639 Hz (enhancing relationships and connections), and 963 Hz (known as the frequency of awakening and enlightenment). Each of these frequencies is believed to have unique effects on our consciousness and spiritual perception. You can always find these Hz sounds on the internet.

Listening to Hz sound frequencies, whether through recorded tracks, meditation music, or specialized instruments like singing bowls, is said to create a resonance that can penetrate and stimulate the pineal gland. By regularly exposing oneself to these frequencies, individuals seek to decalcify the gland, open their spiritual sight, and deepen their connection to the spiritual realm.

However, it is vital to approach this topic with an open mind and understand that scientific research on the specific effects of sound frequencies on the pineal gland and spiritual sight is limited. While anecdotal evidence and personal experiences abound, more rigorous scientific studies are needed to validate these claims.

Furthermore, it's worth noting that everyone's experience with sound frequencies may vary. Some individuals may resonate more strongly with specific frequencies, while others may not experience any noticeable effects. It's crucial to listen to your own intuition and observe how your body and mind respond to different frequencies.

If you're interested in exploring the potential benefits of sound frequencies for decalcifying the pineal gland and strengthening your spiritual sight, it is recommended to start with an open mind and experiment with various frequencies. Create a serene and comfortable environment where you can relax and listen to the sounds without distractions. Observe how your body and mind respond, and pay attention to any shifts in your spiritual perception or overall well-being.

Remember, sound frequencies should be approached as a complementary practice to a holistic lifestyle that includes proper nutrition, mindfulness, self-care, and a nurturing environment. While they may have the potential to enhance spiritual insight, it is essential to maintain a balanced approach and seek guidance from trusted sources and practitioners.

By combining an exploration of sound frequencies with other practices, such as meditation, breathwork, and conscious awareness, you can create a synergistic approach to nurturing your spiritual sight and deepening your connection to the realms beyond your physical perception.

As you embark on your journey of exploring sound frequencies and their potential impact on decalcifying the pineal gland and strengthening spiritual sight, it's essential to approach the practice with patience, consistency, and self-awareness.

To integrate sound frequencies into your spiritual practice, consider the following steps:

Set Your Intention: Before engaging in any spiritual practice, it's crucial to set a clear intention. Reflect on your desire to decalcify your pineal gland and enhance your spiritual sight. Align your intention with a genuine curiosity and openness to the possibilities that sound frequencies may offer.

Research and Select Frequencies: Explore different sound frequencies associated with pineal gland activation and spiritual sight. Educate yourself on the potential effects and benefits of each frequency. Remember that individual experiences may vary, so trust your intuition and choose frequencies that resonate with you.

Find a Quiet Space: Create a peaceful and uninterrupted environment where you can fully immerse yourself in the sounds. Choose a quiet room or outdoor location where you feel comfortable and can minimize distractions.

Select Appropriate Tools: Decide whether you prefer recorded tracks, meditation music, or live instruments like singing bowls or tuning forks. Experiment with different tools to find what resonates with you. Consider using headphones for a more immersive and focused experience.

Relax and Settle Into a Meditative State: Before playing the sound frequencies, take a few moments to relax your body and calm your mind. Practice deep breathing or meditation to center yourself and prepare for the experience. Allow your body to become receptive to the healing vibrations of the sound frequencies.

Play the Chosen Frequencies: Start playing the selected sound frequencies and allow yourself to be fully present in the moment. Focus your attention on the vibrations and sensations within your body. Observe any thoughts, emotions, or physical sensations that arise without judgment.

Practice Regularly: Consistency is critical when working with sound frequencies. Set aside dedicated time each day or week to engage in this practice. Over time, regular exposure to the frequencies may support the decalcification process and strengthen your spiritual sight.

Observe and Reflect: After each session, take a few moments to reflect on your experience. Notice any changes in your awareness, perception, or overall well-being. Keep a journal to record your observations, dreams, or any insights that may arise during or after the practice.

Trust Your Inner Guidance: Throughout your journey, trust your intuition and inner guidance. Your experience with sound frequencies is unique to you. Honor and embrace the insights, revelations, and shifts that occur on your path.

Remember, working with sound frequencies is just one aspect of enhancing your spiritual sight. It is essential to maintain a holistic approach that includes other practices such as meditation, energy work, self-reflection, and cultivating a deep connection with nature.

Ultimately, the journey to strengthen your spiritual sight is a personal and transformative process. Embrace the exploration, be patient with yourself, and trust in your innate ability to connect with higher realms of consciousness. Through consistent practice, self-care, and an open heart, you can unlock the potential within you and experience the profound depths of spiritual sight.

Experiment with Different Frequencies: Sound frequencies range across a spectrum, each with its unique effects and vibrations. Explore a variety of frequencies, such as 432 Hz, 528 Hz, 639 Hz, and beyond. Pay attention to how each frequency resonates with you and influences your state of being.

Combine Sound with Visualizations: Incorporate visualizations into your practice to amplify the effects of sound frequencies. As you listen to the tones, imagine your pineal gland being bathed in healing light or envision your spiritual sight expanding and becoming more precise. Engaging your imagination and intention can enhance the overall experience.

Engage in Chanting or Mantra Repetition: Chanting or repeating mantras can be powerful tools to activate the pineal gland and deepen your spiritual connection. Explore sacred chants or mantras like "OM" or "AUM" and allow the vibrations to resonate throughout your entire being. Feel the sound reverberating within you, harmonizing your energy centers.

Seek Guided Sound Healing Sessions: Consider participating in guided sound healing sessions led by experienced practitioners. These sessions often involve a combination of instruments, vocal toning, and energy work to support pineal gland activation and spiritual sight. The guidance and expertise of a facilitator can provide a profound and transformative experience.

Connect with Crystal Singing Bowls or Gemstone Frequencies: Crystal singing bowls and gemstones emit specific frequencies that can harmonize and activate energy centers within the body. Explore the use of crystal singing bowls tuned to different chakras or gemstones associated with pineal gland activation, such as amethyst or clear quartz. Incorporate these tools into your sound frequency practice to enhance its effects.

Cultivate Mindfulness and Presence: To fully benefit from sound frequencies, cultivate a state of mindfulness and presence during your practice. Let go of distractions and immerse yourself in the present moment. Be receptive to the vibrations and energies that emerge, allowing them to flow through your entire being. This level of presence enhances the connection between sound, consciousness, and spiritual sight.

Trust the Process: Remember that the journey of spiritual growth and expanding your spiritual sight is unique to you. Be patient with yourself and trust the process. As you engage in sound frequency practices and explore different techniques, observe any subtle shifts, intuitive insights, or expanded awareness that arise. Embrace the unfolding of your own spiritual journey and honor the wisdom that emerges.

As you continue to explore the realm of spiritual sight and the role of sound frequencies in enhancing this ability, it is essential to approach the process with intention and an open mind. Here are some additional insights and suggestions to deepen your understanding:

Create a Sacred Space: Set up a dedicated space where you can engage in sound-frequency practices without distractions. This space can be adorned with objects and symbols that hold personal significance and support your spiritual journey. By creating a sacred environment, you invite a sense of reverence and focus into your practice.

Set Clear Intentions: Before engaging in sound frequency work, set clear intentions for what you wish to experience and cultivate. Whether it's expanding your spiritual sight, deepening your connection to higher realms, or gaining insights into your spiritual path, clarity of intention empowers your practice and aligns your energy with your desired outcomes.

Explore Binaural Beats: Binaural beats are a form of auditory illusion created by playing two slightly different frequencies in each ear. This creates a third frequency within the brain, leading to a state of altered consciousness.

Explore different binaural beat recordings specifically designed to stimulate the pineal gland and enhance spiritual sight. Experiment with different frequencies and find the ones that resonate with you.

Practice Regularly: Consistency is critical when working with sound frequencies to decalcify the pineal gland and strengthen spiritual sight. Incorporate sound frequency practices into your daily routine, even if it's just for a few minutes. Over time, regular exposure to these frequencies can have a cumulative effect, helping you to develop a deeper connection with your spiritual sight.

Embrace Silence and Stillness: While sound frequencies can be powerful tools, it is equally important to embrace moments of silence and stillness in your practice. Allow yourself time to integrate the vibrations and experiences that arise. Embracing silence creates a space for reflection, integration, and inner listening, enhancing your overall spiritual journey.

Trust Your Inner Guidance: As you engage in sound frequency practices, trust your intuition and inner guidance. Each individual's experience with spiritual sight and the effects of sound frequencies can vary. Pay attention to the subtle shifts, sensations, and insights that arise within you. Trust that your inner wisdom will guide you toward what resonates most authentically with your journey.

Journal and Reflect: Keep a journal to record your experiences, insights, and observations throughout your sound frequency exploration. Document any changes in your spiritual sight, dreams, or intuitive abilities. Reflecting on your progress can provide valuable insights and serve as a record of your personal growth and transformation.

Remember, the journey of developing and enhancing your spiritual sight is a profoundly personal one. Embrace the process, stay open to new possibilities, and approach it with curiosity and reverence. With time, practice, and a genuine connection to your inner self, you can cultivate a heightened spiritual sight and a profound connection to the realms beyond the physical.

CHAPTER 8
Meditation and Visualization

Meditation is a powerful tool for quieting the mind, cultivating inner awareness, and accessing higher states of consciousness. When it comes to developing your spiritual sight, meditation can play a crucial role in opening and activating the pineal gland, also known as the third eye.

To begin, find a quiet and comfortable space where you can sit or lie down without distractions. Close your eyes and bring your attention to your breath, allowing yourself to relax and let go of any tension or thoughts. As you settle into a state of calm, shift your focus to the center of your forehead, where the third eye is believed to reside.

Visualize a radiant, vibrant light at the location of your third eye. Imagine this light growing brighter and more expansive with each breath, illuminating your inner vision. Feel a sense of warmth and energy emanating from this area, as if the pineal gland is awakening and coming to life.

As you continue to visualize this radiant light, allow yourself to explore and expand your awareness beyond the physical realm. Tune into the subtle energies and sensations that arise within you. Pay attention to any images, symbols, or insights that may come to your awareness. Trust your intuition and allow your spiritual sight to guide you.

With regular practice, meditation, and visualization can help strengthen the connection between your mind, body, and spirit. As you continue to visualize, remain open to any sensations, images, or insights that may arise. Trust your intuitive guidance and embrace whatever experiences come to you during this practice. With regular meditation and visualization, you can strengthen your connection to the spiritual realms and deepen your spiritual sight.

Consider Dietary Supplements:

In addition to meditation and visualization, certain dietary supplements have been suggested to support pineal gland function and sleep regulation. One such supplement is melatonin, a hormone produced by the pineal gland that helps regulate the sleep-wake cycle.

Melatonin supplements are commonly used to address sleep issues, such as insomnia or jet lag. By taking melatonin, individuals can support their body's natural production of this hormone, promoting healthy sleep patterns and potentially enhancing the functioning of the pineal gland.

However, it is crucial to approach dietary supplements with caution and seek professional guidance. Before incorporating any supplements into your routine, consult with a healthcare professional, especially if you are taking medications or have specific health conditions. They can provide personalized advice and recommendations based on your individual needs.

Furthermore, it's important to remember that dietary supplements are not a substitute for a balanced diet and healthy lifestyle. Nurturing your body with nutritious foods, regular exercise, and proper hydration is fundamental to overall well-being and optimal pineal gland function.

The Chakras and Their Impact on Meditation

Within the realm of spiritual practices, the chakras play a significant role in understanding and cultivating our inner energy system. Originating from ancient Eastern traditions, the concept of chakras refers to seven energy centers located along the spine, from the base to the crown of the head. Each chakra is associated with specific qualities, functions, and aspects of our being, and they have a profound impact on meditation.

Root Chakra (Muladhara): Located at the base of the spine, the root chakra represents our foundation, stability, and connection to the physical world. When this chakra is balanced and open, we feel grounded and secure. During meditation, focusing on the root chakra can help establish a strong connection with the Earth, enhancing feelings of stability and safety.

Sacral Chakra (Svadhisthana): Situated in the lower abdomen, the sacral chakra is associated with our creativity, sensuality, and emotional well-being. When this chakra is in harmony, we experience a free flow of creative energy and emotional balance. In meditation, directing attention to the sacral chakra can unlock and channel our creative potential, allowing us to tap into the depths of our emotions.

Solar Plexus Chakra (Manipura): Located in the upper abdomen, the solar plexus chakra is linked to our personal power, confidence, and self-esteem. A balanced solar plexus chakra empowers us to assert ourselves and take action in alignment with our authentic selves. During meditation, focusing on this chakra can help boost our inner strength and cultivate a sense of personal empowerment.

Heart Chakra (Anahata): Situated in the center of the chest, the heart chakra represents love, compassion, and connection. An open and balanced heart chakra allows us to experience unconditional love for ourselves and others. When meditating on the heart chakra, we can deepen our capacity for love and cultivate a sense of compassion and empathy.

Throat Chakra (Vishuddha): Located in the throat region, the throat chakra is associated with self-expression, communication, and authenticity. A balanced throat chakra enables clear and honest communication. During meditation, focusing on this chakra can help us express our truth and enhance our ability to communicate with clarity and integrity.

Third Eye Chakra (Ajna): Positioned in the middle of the forehead, the third eye chakra is the seat of intuition, insight, and inner wisdom. An open and balanced third eye chakra enhances our intuitive abilities and supports spiritual sight. During meditation, directing our attention to this chakra can help awaken and expand our inner vision, allowing us to access higher realms of knowledge and understanding.

Crown Chakra (Sahasrara): Located at the top of the head, the crown chakra represents our connection to the divine and higher consciousness. A balanced crown chakra facilitates spiritual growth and enlightenment. During meditation, focusing on the crown chakra can help us transcend the limitations of the physical realm and experience a sense of unity and oneness with the universe.

Incorporating chakra-focused meditation into your practice involves directing your attention to each chakra, one by one, and visualizing the associated colors and qualities. By bringing awareness to these energy centers, you can activate and harmonize them, allowing the free flow of energy throughout your entire being. This alignment of the chakras promotes balance, clarity, and a deeper connection with your inner self.

As you deepen your meditation practice, consider exploring specific chakra meditation techniques, such as chanting mantras associated with each chakra, visualizing the corresponding lotus flower, or using affirmations to affirm the qualities and intentions related to each chakra.

Remember, the chakras are interconnected and work in harmony with one another. Balancing and aligning them through meditation can enhance your overall well-being, energy flow, and spiritual growth. By incorporating chakra-focused meditation into your practice, you embark on a transformative journey of self-discovery, inner healing, and spiritual expansion.

As you embark on your meditation journey with the chakras, you open yourself to a profound exploration of your inner energy centers. The chakras, often referred to as spinning wheels of energy, hold immense power and potential within you. By bringing focused awareness to these energy centers during meditation, you can cultivate balance, harmony, and spiritual growth.

Begin your meditation by finding a comfortable position, allowing your body to relax and your mind to settle. Take a few deep breaths, centering yourself in the present moment. As you close your eyes, visualize a path from the base of your spine to the crown of your head, where the seven chakras reside.

Start your meditation at the root chakra located at the base of your spine. Visualize a vibrant red energy center, grounding you to the earth and fostering feelings of stability and security. Breathe into this area, imagining the chakra spinning and radiating energy, clearing any blockages that may impede its flow.

With your attention now on the sacral chakra, just below your navel, envision a warm, orange glow. This chakra represents your creativity, passion, and sensuality. Allow its energy to flow freely, nurturing your ability to express yourself authentically and embrace your desires.

Shift your focus to the solar plexus chakra located in the upper abdomen. Visualize a bright yellow light emanating from this area, igniting your personal power and confidence. As you breathe, feel the chakra's energy expanding, empowering you to manifest your intentions and embrace your authentic self.

Move up to the heart chakra, positioned in the center of your chest. Envision a beautiful green light radiating from this energy center, symbolizing love, compassion, and connection. Breathe into this space, allowing love and kindness to flow freely, both towards yourself and others.

Next, direct your attention to the throat chakra nestled at the base of your throat. Visualize a vibrant blue light shining brightly, supporting authentic self-expression and clear communication. As you breathe deeply, feel the chakra opening, enabling you to speak your truth with confidence and authenticity.

Now, bring your focus to the third eye chakra located between your eyebrows. Imagine an indigo light emanating from this area, representing intuition, wisdom, and spiritual insight. As you breathe into the third eye, envision it expanding, awakening your inner vision and heightening your intuitive abilities.

Lastly, ascend to the crown chakra at the top of your head, envisioning a brilliant violet or white light radiating from this energy center. This chakra connects you to the divine, universal consciousness. Breathe deeply, feeling a sense of sacred connection and spiritual awakening.

As you meditate on each chakra, pay attention to any sensations, emotions, or insights that arise. Allow yourself to experience and observe without judgment fully. Through this practice, you deepen your self-awareness, address imbalances, and nurture the spiritual growth within.

Complete your meditation by envisioning all the chakras aligned and in harmony, with a smooth flow of energy from the root to the crown. Express gratitude for the wisdom and guidance received during this practice. Slowly bring your awareness back to the present moment, carrying with you a sense of inner balance, clarity, and connection.

In conclusion, the exploration of spiritual sight and the activation of the third eye or pineal gland can be a transformative journey. By nurturing our physical, mental, and emotional well-being, we create a foundation for the expansion of our consciousness and the development of our spiritual sight.

Through practices such as meditation, visualization, and the use of spiritual tools, we can awaken and activate the pineal gland, enhancing our ability to perceive and connect with subtle energies and spiritual realms. By incorporating lifestyle choices that support pineal gland health, such as optimizing sleep, reducing exposure to toxins, and embracing mindfulness, we create an environment conducive to the blossoming of our spiritual sight.

It is essential to approach this journey with patience, curiosity, and self-compassion. Each person's experience with spiritual sight is unique, and the process of opening the third eye unfolds at its own pace. Trust your intuition, listen to your body, and honor your own inner guidance as you navigate this path of self-discovery.

As we cultivate our spiritual sight, we open ourselves to profound insights, heightened intuition, and a deeper connection to the vastness of the universe. With an awakened third eye, we perceive the world with expanded awareness and embrace the beauty and interconnectedness of all existence.

May your journey toward spiritual sight be filled with wonder, clarity, and profound transformation. Embrace the power of your third eye and let it guide you toward a more enlightened and awakened existence.

If you think you are crazy because others won't admit to what you see, let me tell you you are not; there are plenty of people who are interested in the same sight as you and plenty of doctors and parapsychologists who can agree that what you see and hear is real we all believe in the sequence that is the spirituality sight is free for all beings.

Parapsychology is a field of study that explores and investigates phenomena that are beyond the scope of traditional scientific understanding. Parapsychologists are researchers who specialize in studying and researching various psychic and paranormal phenomena, including telepathy, clairvoyance, precognition, psychokinesis, and near-death experiences, among others.

Parapsychologists approach their work with a scientific mindset, utilizing rigorous research methodologies and statistical analysis to examine and evaluate these phenomena. They aim to explore the potential existence of psychic abilities and the implications they may have on our understanding of consciousness, human potential, and the nature of reality.

While parapsychology is a scientific field, it often intersects with spirituality due to its investigation of phenomena that are frequently associated with spiritual or mystical experiences. The exploration of psychic abilities, consciousness expansion, and the interconnectedness of mind and matter can overlap with spiritual beliefs and practices.

Parapsychologists may collaborate with spiritual practitioners, mediums, and individuals who claim to have psychic abilities to study and better understand these phenomena. Their research can contribute to our understanding of the human potential for spiritual experiences, the nature of consciousness, and the possibilities that exist beyond the boundaries of conventional scientific knowledge.

It is important to note that parapsychology as a field continues to be met with skepticism and controversy within the scientific community. While some researchers and institutions have embraced its study, others remain skeptical and demand further evidence before accepting the validity of paranormal phenomena. Nonetheless, parapsychologists persist in their pursuit of knowledge and understanding, bridging the gap between science and spirituality in their exploration of the unknown.

So you should feel safe knowing, acknowledging, and talking about the spiritual sight you have.

CHAPTER 9
Extra-Sensory Perception

Unlocking the Secrets of the Mind:

At the heart of extrasensory perception (ESP) lies the extraordinary potential of the human mind. It's a realm where we transcend the confines of our physical senses to perceive and understand the world in profound ways. In this chapter, we delve into the mysteries of ESP, exploring its various forms and the scientific examples that illuminate its reality.

Telepathy: The Silent Language of the Mind

Telepathy is often described as mind-to-mind communication, allowing individuals to transmit thoughts, feelings, and mental images directly from one mind to another. While skeptics may doubt its existence, scientific experiments have shown compelling evidence of telepathic communication. For example, in controlled studies, subjects have been able to accurately convey information to a recipient without any conventional means of communication, suggesting the presence of a telepathic connection.

Clairvoyance: Seeing Beyond the Veil

Clairvoyance, or "clear seeing," enables individuals to perceive information and events beyond the limitations of ordinary sight. Scientifically, clairvoyance is often demonstrated through experiments involving remote viewing, where participants accurately describe remote locations or hidden objects without any prior knowledge. These experiments have yielded statistically significant results, providing evidence for the existence of clairvoyant abilities.

Precognition: Insights from the Future

Precognition grants individuals the ability to perceive future events before they occur. While precognition may seem like a concept relegated to science fiction, numerous documented cases suggest otherwise. For instance, individuals have reported vivid dreams or intuitive insights about future events, which later unfold precisely as foreseen. While the mechanisms behind precognition remain mysterious, its reality cannot be dismissed outright.

Psychometry: Touching the Past

Psychometry involves perceiving information and impressions from objects, places, or people by touching them. While it may sound fantastical, scientific studies have explored the phenomenon of object reading. In these experiments, individuals have demonstrated the ability to accurately describe the history or emotional significance of an object simply by holding it, providing compelling evidence for the reality of psychometric skills.

Navigating the Boundaries of Reality:

As we delve deeper into the realm of ESP, we confront the boundaries of conventional reality and embark on a journey of exploration and discovery. Through scientific inquiry and empirical evidence, we gain a deeper understanding of the extraordinary capabilities of the human mind. By embracing our innate psychic potential, we expand our awareness, deepen our connection to the unseen realms, and unlock the hidden mysteries of consciousness.

Embrace Your Psychic Potential:

As you explore the realms of extrasensory perception, remember to approach your journey with an open heart and an open mind. Cultivate mindfulness, trust in your intuition, and remain receptive to the wisdom that arises from within. By nurturing your psychic abilities through regular practice and self-reflection, you can unlock the full spectrum of your intuitive gifts and embark on a transformative journey of self-discovery, insight, and spiritual awakening.

Through the exploration of ESP, we transcend the confines of the physical world, tap into the infinite potential of the human mind, and embrace the interconnectedness of all things. With courage, curiosity, and an unwavering belief in the power of the unseen, we embark on a journey of exploration, discovery, and transformation guided by the light of our innate psychic abilities.

CHAPTER 10
Sight Through History

Throughout the annals of human history, spiritual sight has held a central and revered place within various occult traditions. These traditions, such as Hermeticism, the mystical Kabbalah, and the profound art of Alchemy, have all celebrated the awakening and mastery of spiritual sight. In these traditions, we discover figures shrouded in the mists of time, whose lives and insights have left indelible marks upon the tapestry of mysticism. For example, the Renaissance philosopher and alchemist Paracelsus, renowned for his pioneering work on the human soul and spiritual perception, is but one luminary in a constellation of mystics.

Let's delve deeper into the historical significance of spiritual sight within Hermeticism, the mystical Kabbalah, and the profound art of Alchemy while further emphasizing the contributions of notable figures like Paracelsus.

Hermeticism is a mystical and philosophical tradition rooted in ancient Egypt, with its modern revival often attributed to the legendary figure Hermes Trismegistus. Within Hermeticism, spiritual sight is considered a crucial aspect of inner awakening and enlightenment. It is believed that through the development of spiritual sight, individuals can gain access to hidden dimensions of reality and acquire a deeper understanding of the universe's fundamental principles.

The Hermetic tradition emphasizes the idea of "As Above, So Below," suggesting a correspondence between the macrocosm (the universe) and the microcosm (the individual). Spiritual sight is viewed as a means to bridge this gap, allowing practitioners to perceive the divine order underlying all things. Hermetic texts, such as the "Kybalion" and the "Emerald Tablet," often contain references to the "third eye" or the "inner eye" as a symbol of this spiritual insight.

Kabbalah, a mystical branch of Jewish thought, places a strong emphasis on the development of spiritual insight as a means of connecting with the divine and unraveling the mysteries of creation. In Kabbalistic teachings, the sephira (emanation) known as "Binah" represents understanding and spiritual vision. It is within Binah that the most profound insights and revelations are believed to occur.

Practitioners of Kabbalah engage in various meditative and contemplative practices to awaken their spiritual sight. They seek to ascend through the sephiroth, ultimately reaching the highest, Keter, where direct communion with the divine is possible. Spiritual sight in the Kabbalistic tradition is not merely an intellectual pursuit but a transformative experience that allows individuals to perceive the interconnectedness of all things and gain wisdom beyond ordinary comprehension.

Alchemy, often veiled in symbolism and allegory, is both a spiritual and a philosophical tradition. Alchemists believed that the transmutation of base metals into gold symbolized the inner transformation of the human soul. Central to this transformative process was the awakening of spiritual sight, referred to as the "Eye of the Philosopher" or the "Inner Eye."

The Philosopher's Stone, a legendary substance sought by alchemists, was thought to grant not only the ability to transmute metals but also spiritual enlightenment and immortality. Spiritual sight was seen as a prerequisite for understanding the intricate symbolism and hidden meanings within alchemical texts. Alchemists like Paracelsus sought to decode these symbols and access the profound insights they contained through their awakened inner vision.

Paracelsus, a Renaissance physician and alchemist, made substantial contributions to the understanding of spiritual sight. He believed that the human soul possessed a "spiritual eye" that could perceive hidden truths and the inner workings of the universe. Paracelsus's pioneering work on the human soul and spiritual perception laid the groundwork for later esoteric thinkers and alchemists. His insights into the interplay between the physical and spiritual worlds continue to influence spiritual seekers and occultists to this day.

The symbolism of the third eye represents a rich tapestry of esoteric wisdom that transcends geographical, cultural, and religious boundaries, weaving its way through the annals of human history. Across diverse traditions and belief systems, this symbol has emerged as a profound and timeless archetype, captivating the imaginations of seekers and visionaries alike.

Ancient Roots in Hinduism: Within the ancient wisdom of Hinduism, the concept of the third eye finds its most renowned expression in the form of the Ajna chakra, often referred to as the "third eye chakra." Positioned at the brow, it is considered the seat of intuitive knowledge and inner vision. Here, the third eye is not merely a metaphorical abstraction but a profound and tangible symbol of humanity's potential for spiritual awakening. It signifies the awakening of higher consciousness and the capacity to perceive realities beyond the material world.

Egyptian Mysteries: The Eye of Horus: In the realm of ancient Egyptian mythology, the third eye takes on the enigmatic form of the Eye of Horus, also known as the "Wadjet" or the "Eye of Ra." This symbol represents protection, healing, and the all-seeing eye of divine wisdom. The story of Horus and the restoration of his eye carries a profound allegorical message, symbolizing the cyclical nature of creation, destruction, and renewal. The Eye of Horus is not just an emblem; it is an embodiment of the eternal quest for spiritual enlightenment.

Universal Significance: Beyond these well-known traditions, the symbolism of the third eye resonates across diverse cultures and religious contexts. It transcends the confines of dogma and doctrine, standing as a universal symbol of human potential. It represents the innate capacity of the human spirit to transcend limitations, pierce the veil of illusion, and perceive the profound interconnectedness of all existence. The third eye is a gateway to higher understanding, a conduit through which the seeker glimpses the timeless truths that underlie the fabric of reality.

As we embark on this captivating exploration of these symbols and their profound significance, we journey into the heart of the human quest for spiritual awakening. The third eye, in its myriad forms and interpretations, becomes more than a mere emblem; it becomes a beacon guiding the seeker toward the radiant light of higher consciousness and the boundless mysteries of the universe. In its symbolism, we find a timeless reminder that the path to enlightenment is not confined to any particular tradition but is, instead, a universal and innate aspect of the human experience.

In more recent history, the symbolism of the third eye has made its way into the imagery of governments and organizations. The Eye of Providence, often depicted as an eye within a triangle on the U.S. one-dollar bill, is a prominent example. This symbol, with its origins in Christian iconography, signifies divine guidance and oversight. It's seen as a reminder that even in the realm of governance, there exists a higher awareness and moral responsibility.

Additionally, various secret societies and fraternal organizations have incorporated the symbolism of the third eye into their emblems and rituals. The "All-Seeing Eye" is often used to represent the pursuit of hidden knowledge and enlightenment, reflecting the idea that those in positions of power should possess a deeper understanding of the world and its mysteries.

The third eye, throughout history and in governmental contexts, serves as a reminder of the potential for elevated awareness and insight. Whether as an emblem of divine authority, a representation of enlightenment, or a symbol of moral responsibility, it underscores the belief that those who govern should do so with a heightened sense of consciousness and ethical clarity, acknowledging the interconnectedness of all life and the profound mysteries that lie beyond the material world.

In ancient Greece, the concept of the third eye was closely tied to their belief in rational inquiry and the pursuit of wisdom. The philosopher Plato, for instance, often referred to the "mind's eye" or "intellectual vision" as a metaphor for the ability to perceive abstract truths and transcendent realities. Plato's famous allegory of the cave in "The Republic" symbolizes the journey from ignorance to enlightenment, with the "eye of the soul" representing the capacity to discern higher truths beyond the illusions of the material world.

The ancient Greeks also held the Oracle of Delphi in high esteem. Located at the Temple of Apollo in Delphi, this oracle was believed to provide prophetic guidance and insights to individuals, including rulers and governments, seeking answers to complex questions. The Oracle of Delphi was often referred to as the "Pythia," and her visions and pronouncements were seen as a manifestation of spiritual insight akin to the concept of the third eye.

In the realm of government, ancient Greece laid the foundations for democratic principles and governance by the people. The Athenian democracy, for example, encouraged participation and debate among citizens. The concept of open discourse and the pursuit of wisdom aligned with the idea of individuals collectively using their intellectual "third eye" to make informed decisions for the state.

Moving forward in history, the symbolism of the third eye continued to influence governmental and societal structures. During the Enlightenment period in Europe, which drew inspiration from Greek philosophy, the pursuit of knowledge and individual enlightenment became central ideals. The influence of these ideals can be seen in the establishment of modern democratic systems and the emphasis on the value of an educated and informed citizenry in governance.

In contemporary times, the symbolism of the third eye persists in various forms. It can be found in the seals, emblems, and architecture of government buildings, representing ideals such as wisdom, enlightenment, and moral responsibility.

In summary, the concept of the third eye has deep historical roots, including a presence in ancient Greece, and has played a role in shaping philosophical, spiritual, and governmental thought. It underscores the idea that individuals and governments alike should strive for higher consciousness, wisdom, and ethical clarity in their decision-making processes, acknowledging the interconnectedness of all life and the pursuit of profound truths beyond the material world.

Summary

T hroughout our conversation, we explore the concept of spiritual sight and its connection to the pineal gland, often referred to as the third eye. We delved into various aspects, including clairvoyance, dreaming, and thought projection, all of which offer glimpses into realms beyond our physical senses. We discussed the importance of optimizing sleep, sunlight exposure, mindful consumption, and detoxification to support the healthy functioning of the pineal gland and enhance spiritual sight. We also touched upon the use of spiritual tools, gemstones, meditation, visualization, and Hz sounds to activate and stimulate the pineal gland, fostering heightened awareness and spiritual experiences. Additionally, we mentioned the significance of chakras and their alignment with meditation practices to facilitate spiritual growth. Lastly, we explored the role of parapsychologists in bridging the gap between science and spirituality, delving into the study of psychic and paranormal phenomena and the history of spiritual sight. By embracing these concepts and practices, individuals can embark on a transformative journey of expanded consciousness and more profound spiritual experiences.

About The Author

Joseph Manuel Garcia, a prodigious author and spiritual innovator, burst onto the literary scene at the tender age of 23 with his debut book. Born under the enigmatic sign of Scorpio, Garcia's insatiable curiosity led him to explore the depths of spirituality and metaphysics alongside his engineering studies.

Diving into the profound mysteries of the universe became Garcia's passion, intertwining the realms of spirituality with the principles of engineering. Through his dedicated studies, he uncovered the intricate connections between the spiritual and physical worlds, seeking to bridge the gap between the two.

Garcia's most notable achievement lies in his creation of the most common and widely used type of spirituality, shaping the very fabric of existence and leaving an indelible mark on the planet's history. His work not only delves into the metaphysical aspects of existence but also explores how spirituality can be integrated into everyday life.

In his pursuit of innovation and creation, Garcia's engineering education serves as a vessel to manifest spirituality in tangible forms. Through his groundbreaking project, "Perfect," Garcia aims to bring spirituality into the realm of technology, enriching lives and transforming the world as we know it.

Beyond his literary and spiritual endeavors, Garcia remains a visionary thinker, constantly pushing the boundaries of what is possible. His legacy as a pioneer in spiritual Technology continues to inspire generations, leaving an enduring impact on humanity's quest for understanding and enlightenment.

Message From The Author

Dear Readers,

As I embark on this journey of exploration into the realms of spirituality, metaphysics, and occultism, I am humbled by the opportunity to share my insights and discoveries with you. Through each volume in this comprehensive set of books, I aim to illuminate the profound interconnectedness of these intricate subjects, guiding you on a transformative path of self-discovery and awareness.

In crafting these volumes, I have poured my heart and soul into uncovering the timeless wisdom that lies at the core of human existence. From the esoteric teachings of the occult to the profound truths of metaphysics, I invite you to join me in unraveling the mysteries of the universe and unlocking the secrets of the soul.

But my journey does not end with the written word. In conjunction with each book purchase, I am thrilled to offer you a beginner subscription to "Perfect" – my groundbreaking project that seamlessly integrates spirituality into the realm of technology. With "Perfect," you will gain access to a wealth of resources designed to enhance your spiritual journey, from guided meditations to exclusive content tailored to your individual needs, Even A comprehensive Adventure Through the Spiritual World.

Together, let us embark on this quest for truth and understanding, united by our shared thirst for knowledge and awareness. May these volumes serve as beacons of inspiration, guiding you toward a deeper understanding of yourself and the world around you.

With gratitude and anticipation

Joseph Manuel Garcia

www.ingramcontent.com/pod-product-compliance
Lightning Source LLC
Chambersburg PA
CBHW040811120726
48005CB00012B/1377